EXCELLING IN
FOOTBALL

By Matt Scheff

ReferencePoint
Press®

San Diego, CA

For more information, contact:
ReferencePoint Press, Inc.
PO Box 27779
San Diego, CA 92198
www.ReferencePointPress.com

LIBRARY OF CONGRESS CATALOGING-IN-PUBLICATION DATA

Names: Scheff, Matt, author.
Title: Excelling in football / by Matt Scheff.
Description: San Diego, California : ReferencePoint Press, Inc., [2020] |
    Series: Teen Guide to Sports | Audience: Grades: 9 to 12. | Includes
    bibliographical references and index.
Identifiers: LCCN 2019005375 (print) | LCCN 2019009879 (ebook) | ISBN
    9781682827000 (ebook) | ISBN 9781682826997 (hardcover)
Subjects: LCSH: Football--Training--United States--Juvenile literature. |
    Football players--Health and hygiene--Juvenile literature. | Football
    players--United States--Conduct of life--Juvenile literature. | Football
    players--Vocational guidance--United States--Juvenile literature. |
    National Football League--Juvenile literature.
Classification: LCC GV953.5 (ebook) | LCC GV953.5 .S35 2020 (print) | DDC
    796.332--dc23
LC record available at https://lccn.loc.gov/2019005375

CONTENTS

HOW DO PLAYERS
MAKE THE TEAM?

It's the middle of summer, and Javier has one thing on his mind: football. He loves the game and everything about it. It's the crunching of shoulder pads. It's the sight of the ball sailing through the air. It's the smell of the turf and the crispness of the air. It's the thrill of a touchdown, the excitement of a big tackle, and the roar of the crowd. There's nothing like it.

> **"There are no shortcuts. If you want to be successful, you've got to put the time in with your training. I want high-intensity training, every single day."[1]**
>
> *– Larry Fitzgerald, Arizona Cardinals wide receiver*

Watching football from the stands is great, but this year, Javier wants more. He wants to be on the field, playing alongside his friends and classmates. He dreams of scoring the big touchdown, making a game-saving tackle, or booting a field goal through the uprights.

There are many steps before players get to tryouts. Preparation is crucial to making the team.

It won't be easy, though. Making the football team will take hard work. What will it take for Javier to prepare? He looks to his National Football League (NFL) heroes to find out. According to Arizona Cardinals wide receiver Larry Fitzgerald, it's all about hard work. "There are no shortcuts," says Fitzgerald. "If you want to be successful, you've got to put the time in with your training. I want high-intensity training, every single day."[1]

Carolina Panthers linebacker Luke Kuechly says working out is only part of the process. "You can work as hard as you want inside a facility, and your program can be great, but if you don't balance it with a quality nutrient plan, you're going to have some issues," he says. "No matter how hard you work [on the field], it's also what you do when you're not in here."[2]

"It's natural for me to want fast food and sweet tea, but those are the things I've had to cut back on. It's been hard, but in order to be the best player I can be on the field, I had to limit them or completely cut them out."[3]

– Deshaun Watson, Houston Texans quarterback

"It's natural for me to want fast food and sweet tea, but those are the things I've had to cut back on," says Houston Texans quarterback Deshaun Watson. "It's been hard, but in order to be the best player I can be on the field, I had to limit them or completely cut them out."[3]

A fit body and heathy diet are good places to start. But on the football field, skills are just as important. "To create stronger, faster connections in our brains, we need to practice a habit, skill, or behavior again and again," says legendary New England Patriots quarterback Tom Brady. "The more we practice that habit, skill, or behavior, the more automatically our brains recognize it."[4]

Even great physical conditioning and sharp skills aren't enough, according to former NFL defensive end Ryan Riddle. Preparing the mind is just as important. "If you're unable to mentally prepare yourself for this high stress, incredibly competitive environment, there's little chance for you to have [success]," Riddle says.[5]

Many players use visualization to prepare their minds. They imagine themselves catching the ball, making a tackle, or booting a long kick. San Francisco 49ers defensive back Richard Sherman says, "I try to remember the moments when I was at my best—when I was having a great day and I really was in my zone. I go back to that feeling. Then I attack the day. I attack the game with that same enthusiasm."[6]

Javier soaks in all of the tips. He begins a healthful diet and starts exercising. He runs. He lifts weights. He studies how the best players in the world work on and off the field. He practices his skills and tries to learn from his mistakes. He also prepares his mind, building a positive mental attitude. Javier lists each of his goals on a piece of paper and attaches it to his bedroom door. He looks at them every morning as a way to help motivate himself to keep working.

> **"I try to remember the moments when I was at my best—when I was having a great day and I really was in my zone. I go back to that feeling. Then I attack the day. I attack the game with that same enthusiasm."[6]**
>
> *– Richard Sherman, San Francisco 49ers cornerback*

The day of tryouts finally arrives. The sounds of coaches' whistles fill the air as Javier steps onto the field. He's ready to show off his hard work, training, and mental preparation. These are the hurdles football players at every level face—from high school to the pros. It takes preparation at every level, from proper nutrition and exercise to skills training and getting into in a winning frame of mind. Every step helps him grow stronger and tougher. It's what he needs to make the team.

"You need to have some talent to play," says Green Bay Packers linebacker Clay Matthews. "But if you're willing to work and put in the time and effort, you'll have a better chance [at succeeding at your level] than someone with just raw talent. You're going to be more likely to make a team and make an impact on the field [if you're a hard worker]."[7]

CHAPTER ONE

HOW CAN PLAYERS PREPARE
FOR TRYOUTS?

Tryouts are where high school football teams are built. Coaches and players swarm the field. Players are drilled, measured, and challenged as coaches figure out who has what it takes—and who doesn't. But the process of making the team starts long before tryout day. Players who want an edge spend months preparing, getting their minds and bodies ready for their shot to make the team. That way, when the time comes to step onto the field and show their skills, they've got every advantage.

SETTING GOALS

Some players can show up to tryouts and get by on raw, natural athletic ability or skill. But for most players, it's a long process of building up the body. It can be easy for players to lose focus or fall behind. This is where setting goals comes into play. Setting concrete goals gives players very specific milestones to work toward and can help keep them focused over months of preparation. Some goals may be small—such as doing 100 push-ups a day, getting eight hours of sleep, or avoiding sweets. Others will be more difficult and take a long time. Detroit Lions linebacker Devon Kennard calls these goals stretch goals.

Coaches evaluate players at tryouts. They look at what position players might play, what the team needs, and even each players' academics.

"A stretch goal is a goal that is going to make you uncomfortable but, at the same time, it's a goal that is attainable," Kennard says. "Whatever career you're in, whatever you're trying to accomplish in your life, set the stretch goals and actually have a plan to achieve it."[8]

When he was in seventh grade, Kennard had several long-term stretch goals. One of them was to play in the NFL. Kennard wrote down his goals and posted them to his bathroom wall. That way, he saw the goals every day. He couldn't forget them. Kennard's approach is just one way of setting goals. But many experts agree that writing down your goals can be helpful. For many people, writing down a goal helps make it more real and keeps their focus on it.

Every player should ask himself what his goals are. He should identify both short-term and long-term goals. The goals should be challenging but achievable. Setting a goal that cannot be met will lead to frustration. Players might give up if they feel their goals are impossible. For the most challenging goals, players may set up progress goals to achieve along the way. For example, if a player sets a goal of running a mile in less than six minutes, he might break down the goal into a series of goals. The first step could be to do it in seven minutes. Then six minutes, thirty seconds, and so on. Each goal builds on the previous one.

People will have different goals. A lineman may focus on strength-based goals, while a defensive back may focus on speed and agility. A kicker or punter might focus on flexibility and mental focus, while a quarterback might be more concerned with arm strength and studying the playbook. Players need to be well-rounded, but the important thing is to have goals and to continually work toward them.

"A body isn't made overnight. It's a progression of hard work and dedication, so it starts with square one. One hour of cardio and one hour of weights, four days a week. And you've gotta have a rest day."[9]

– DeMarcus Ware, former Denver Broncos defensive end

WORKOUTS AND CONDITIONING

Football is rough, tough, and fast-paced. Players need to be in peak physical condition to compete. One of the biggest parts of preparing for tryouts is conditioning. A workout program helps each player improve his strength, agility, stamina, and flexibility.

It takes hard work, according to former defensive lineman DeMarcus Ware. "A body isn't made overnight," he says. "It's a progression of hard work and dedication, so it starts with square one. One hour of cardio and one hour of weights, four days a week. And you've gotta have a rest day."[9]

STRETCHING

Most fitness experts agree that one part of a workout that no one should skip is stretching. It's not the flashiest or most exciting part of a workout. But stretching helps to prepare muscles for what's to come, and it helps reduce the chances of injury during a game or workout. Just a few minutes of stretching can make all the difference.

"We do these old school stretches—heavy, heavy squats with chains, a lot of flexibility, a lot of warming up when a lot of people in the NFL skip warming up," said former San Francisco 49ers safety Donte Whitner. "That's why we have a good, healthy football team right now."[10]

It's important to stretch all of the muscle groups that will be used in a workout, from the calves and quadriceps to the latissimus and deltoids. It doesn't have to take long, but it's important. Having muscles that are properly stretched can be the key to staying healthy in the weight room and on the field.

There are different kinds of stretches. Two of the most popular ways to stretch are static and dynamic. Static stretches involve stretching a muscle and holding it for period of time. One example is the popular quadriceps stretch. The player grabs the foot behind the body while standing and maintains the hold to stretch the quadriceps in the front of the leg. Dynamic stretches are done in motion. An example of dynamic stretching would be the single-leg dead lift.

The person stands on one leg and leans forward, moving the other leg back so that the body and raised leg make a line parallel to the ground. The person touches the ground as he or she bends over. This stretches the hamstring in the back of the thigh and forces the person to maintain balance. The person returns to a standing position after touching the ground.

CARDIO

One of the cornerstones of any workout plan is cardiovascular exercise. It is often called cardio. Cardio is any type of exercise that elevates the heart rate over a period of time. The heart is a muscle, and cardio strengthens it. It also helps the lungs and circulatory system.

One of the most common cardio workouts is running or jogging. Running as fast as possible isn't the idea. Rather, it's about setting a pace that one can keep up for a long period of time. Cardio workouts build over time. People who are just starting may only be able to jog for five or ten minutes. As they build cardio conditioning, they will be able to run for even longer. Many NFL players do cardio for an hour or more at a time.

Running isn't the only option, however. Anything that increases the heart rate will work. Biking, jumping rope, climbing stairs, swimming, or even just brisk walking all serve as cardio workouts.

UPPER BODY AND CORE WORKOUTS

Upper body strength is a must for almost all positions in football. That's especially true for linemen, running backs, and linebackers. Some players build their upper body strength in the weight room. However, many people prefer to work out beyond the weight room.

Cardio is one part of preparing for the game that every player can work on. Players can improve their cardio capacity by running.

Push-ups are a classic upper body workout. They build strength in the arm, shoulder, back, and chest muscles. Other good arm workouts include pull-ups, chin-ups, and dips. Some players work with heavy medicine balls.

Core strength might be even more important. Strength through the back and abdomen gives the body stability and helps protect against injuries. Many people build their core strength through sit-ups or crunches. Leg raises are another great core workout. To do leg raises, a person lays flat on the back and raises the heels a few inches off of the ground, without bending the knees. Then he slowly raises the legs until they are straight up. Planks are exercises in which a person holds the body flat while resting on the elbows and toes. All of these are workouts players can do almost anywhere, without equipment.

LEG WORKOUTS

Most football players generate their power and momentum through their legs, so lower body strength is critical. "When you're growing up, you always think that your upper body strength and everybody is testing your best thing, your bench max and all that kind of stuff," says Seattle Seahawks quarterback Russell Wilson. "As a quarterback, it's really more so leg strength, core strength, shoulder stability, and core stability. The thing that I really pride myself on is . . . my mobility and flexibility. I'm constantly working out those areas."[11]

Players can build leg strength in different ways. Some lift weights. They do leg presses, squats, and deadlifts. Leg presses are an exercise in which a person pushes weight away from them with their legs. For a squat, a person holds a kettlebell or barbell and bends at the knees, and then straightens the legs. Deadlifts start with a barbell on the ground. A person lowers the hips to pick up the barbell. The back is kept straight and the hips come forward as the person stands.

Many people prefer to get leg workouts outside of the weight room using exercises such as lunges. Lunges don't require any equipment and offer a great workout. A person starts from a standing position, with the feet waist length apart. Then he takes a long step forward, bending the leg so that the heel hits the floor first. The step should be long enough that the knee is bent at 90 degrees. The heel pushes the leg back up, and the cycle starts again. Some people work on one leg at a time during lunges. Others alternate legs.

Stairs are another great way to work out the lower body. Running stairs combines the benefits of cardio with the strengthening of the legs. Players can either run up and down real stairs or use a stair climber machine.

JERRY RICE'S CLIMBING WORKOUT

Few players in NFL history have had better careers than Hall of Fame wide receiver Jerry Rice. He is considered one of the best receivers of all time. He set many of the all-time receiving records in the NFL and won three Super Bowls with the San Francisco 49ers. Rice's lower-body strength and conditioning were legendary. He owed much of his success to a simple workout that almost anyone could try—Rice ran up hills.

Every day during the off-season, Rice and teammate Roger Craig met at a local nature preserve and ran up a hill. "The main thing for me was conditioning, and it started with this hill," Rice said. "We did this, and it's what made us capable of outdoing everybody else during the football season. It was about being able to put your body through pain."

Hill running is great cardio as well as a lower-body workout. It can help players get faster and gain leg strength. If the hill is in a remote area, it is best to run with a friend or teammate.

Quoted in Zac Clark, "Jerry Rice's Legendary Hill Training," Stack, October 17, 2010. www.stack.com.

CROSS-TRAINING

Targeted exercise can be helpful. But another way to work out is cross-training. In cross-training, a person exercises by doing another sport or activity. Popular activities football players do to stay in shape include swimming, biking, yoga, basketball, and rock climbing. Cross-training is an important part of working out. It works muscle groups in different ways and combinations. It also helps to keep workouts fun. Boredom leads to athletes not focusing on technique or pushing themselves to get better. An athlete who is bored with certain types of exercise can still get a great workout by cross-training. This is best kept to the off-season to help keep the player in shape. Off-season cross-training should focus on core stability, aerobic capacity, and flexibility.

Many players have spent time running stairs to improve cardio and leg strength. Players often run the stairs in the football stadium, but stairs anywhere will work.

"After years of doing the same mundane football workouts . . . [cross-training] was something new," says former NFL linebacker Dhani Jones. "It didn't feel like work. I was enjoying it."[12]

CROSS-TRAINING FOCUS

By strengthening the core, the rest of the body is able to move strongly and efficiently. It creates a good base for muscles and joints during workouts and games. This keeps joints safe and helps the player to provide power in his movements. Good ways to cross-train for the core include gymnastics, yoga, and Pilates.

Aerobic capacity is the ability of an athlete's muscles to use oxygen and continue working. This correlates with endurance and conditioning. Other workouts can provide players with anaerobic

YOGA

More and more NFL players are turning to yoga, not just as a workout but as a way to prepare their minds and bodies for game day. Yoga is a low-impact exercise that focuses on quieting the mind and stretching the muscles. During yoga, people perform and hold poses that promote flexibility and mindfulness. Both can be beneficial before a game. "Yoga has played a big part in my life and career, because it works my mind and body," says Carolina Panthers safety Mike Adams.

Players interested in trying yoga can search for classes in their area. They can also go online to search for a wide range of yoga videos. Many are suitable for beginners, and players who try them may just find a new weapon to prepare both their bodies and minds for the football field.

Quoted in *"Players Turning to Yoga as a Way to Stay in Shape,"* New York Times, *August 29, 2015.* *www.nytimes.com.*

exercise, which instead involves big bursts of movement, but cross-training with jogging, swimming, or cycling can help a player with his conditioning to stay fresh in games.

Flexibility comes in two forms, passive and dynamic. Passive flexibility refers to a person's range of motion. To an extent, all athletes need passive flexibility. Athletes also need a certain amount of dynamic flexibility depending on their sport and position. This is the ability for certain muscles to relax and not interfere with the movement of other muscles. An example of this is the flexibility needed by defensive ends when they rush around the outside of a pocket. They need to be able to engage the offensive tackle and get below the tackle's leverage. To move like this the inside and outside muscle groups need to work together. This affects the ankles, knees, and hips during a pass rush. It can be noticed in how much a defensive end dips his hips and inside shoulder.

BEFORE THE TRYOUT

Tryout day is almost here. How does an athlete prepare? There's no one way to do it, but many athletes follow some basic guidelines. Many take off the day before a big tryout or game. They give their bodies a chance to rest and rebuild. Others will do a light workout instead of a full session in the gym.

The night before the tryout, players eat complex carbohydrates, such as pasta or potatoes. Complex carbs will give them extra energy the following day by providing muscles with plenty of glycogen. Glycogen is a fuel used by muscles for anaerobic exercise.

Sleep is critical. A good night's sleep before the tryout will leave the body rested and the mind sharp. Lack of sleep slows reaction times and leaves athletes sluggish. Eight to ten solid hours of sleep per night is a good goal.

Atlanta Falcons quarterback Matt Ryan believes proper rest is even more important than time at the practice facility. Early in his career, Ryan said he tried to be the first player to work every morning. But he learned that it was more important to rest than it was to start working at the crack of dawn. "I thought that [going in early] showed dedication and work ethic," Ryan said. "I don't do that anymore, because I realized it is more important to be rested and ready than it is to beat everybody to work."[13]

> **"I thought that [going in early] showed dedication and work ethic. I don't do that anymore, because I realized it is more important to be rested and ready than it is to beat everybody to work."[13]**
>
> *– Matt Ryan, Atlanta Falcons quarterback*

THE BIG DAY

Every coach runs tryouts a little differently. Coaches all have

18

their own styles and different ways of evaluating players. But most tryouts share some common features. Knowing what to expect will make tryouts less stressful and prepare players to be at their best.

Often, the first and most basic part of a tryout is a player's measurements. Coaches record each player's height and weight. Many also have players do a standing broad jump. From a standing start, players jump as far as they can, and the distance is recorded. These basic measurements help coaches decide where on the field each player might be best suited to play.

Coaches test players' strength, speed, skills, and physical condition by putting them through drills. One of the most commonly run drills is the 40-yard (37-m) dash. It's a simple but important drill. Players have to run 40 yards as quickly as they can. There's no substitute for speed. The dash is how a coach can measure a player's ability to keep up. The fastest NFL players run the 40-yard dash in less than 4.4 seconds. In 2017, Cincinnati Bengals wide receiver John Ross ran it in 4.22 seconds. That is the fastest time ever recorded at the NFL Combine, a tryout for college players hoping to enter the NFL. Most NFL linemen run the dash in approximately five seconds. High school coaches don't hold players to NFL standards. The important thing to remember is that the more a position depends on speed, the more a good 40 time will impress coaches.

Speed is good, but football players also need quickness and agility. Coaches use a number of drills to test these abilities. In one drill, coaches place three cones in an *L* shape, five yards (4.6 m) apart from each other. Players start at an end cone. They sprint to the middle cone, touch it, turn and sprint back to the cone they started at, then sprint out to the middle cone, turn, and dip inside the last cone. They finish by sprinting back around the middle cone and back to

Coaches record players' results in drills. This includes timing the 40-yard (37 m) dash and three-cone drill.

the starting place. In this drill, raw speed isn't the key. It's the ability to quickly run, change directions, and accelerate again. According to one NFL scout, the three-cone drill is "the single most important drill, plain and simple. Regardless of position, I want to know how the player performs in space and this helps show change of direction, explosiveness, and overall athleticism."[14]

Strength is key for many positions in football. At a tryout, coaches evaluate strength in a number of ways. One of them is to have players hit a tackling dummy or a blocking sled. They can see how hard they hit and how fast they can push a heavy weight. This can determine if a player will be a linebacker or lineman.

Players will be sorted into positions to run separate drills. They are expected to execute them. Coaches may break teams into offensive and defensive units to run these drills together. This makes the tryouts more efficient and helps coaches see which players understand their jobs and which players struggle.

> "Attitude is number one. It doesn't matter if you're not the best athlete in the world. We look for that person who keeps getting back up and getting after it. If they have that drive, I know I can win with that person. It's hard to cut a person who's giving everything he's got and putting it all on the line."[15]
>
> – Jim Ledford, high school football coach

Physical skills are important. But they don't mean anything without football skills. Coaches will want to measure how well a player can throw, catch, block, kick, and tackle. They run one-on-one drills to evaluate each of these skills. A player's body type will have a big impact on which sorts of drills they're asked to do. Larger players may be asked to block each other. More slender players may be asked to block, throw, and catch. Every coach runs different drills in different ways. But players should expect drills that test their on-field skills. It's their chance to show off the results of all the hard work they've done in preparation. Good technique here is key.

Drills will help coaches decide which players make the team. But they're only a piece of the puzzle. According to Jim Ledford, head coach at Berkner High School in Richardson, Texas, a player's frame of mind is very important. "Attitude is number one," Ledford says. "It doesn't matter if you're not the best athlete in the world. We look for that person who keeps getting back up and getting after it. If they have that drive, I know I can win with that person. It's hard to cut a person who's giving everything he's got and putting it all on the line."[15]

CHAPTER TWO

HOW CAN PLAYERS PREPARE
THEIR BODIES?

Working out during the off-season is important. But it takes a lot more to maintain success on the field. To excel in football, a player needs to fuel his body with the proper nutrition. He also must constantly work to keep his football skills sharp.

Many NFL players believe that proper nutrition is the key to success on the field. Eating right is important for everyone. But for an athlete who is working out for several hours multiple days a week, getting the proper fuel is critical. Many NFL players focus on eating high-protein diets mixed with carbohydrates and fats. They avoid junk food and empty calories, or foods with little nutritional value. Striking the right balance gives a player the building blocks he needs to succeed.

"Every time we put something in our body, we have a chemical reaction and either it's a good reaction or a bad reaction," says wide receiver Brandon Marshall. "It's a weapon for us—it fuels us, gives us energy, it helps us

> **"Every time we put something in our body, we have a chemical reaction and either it's a good reaction or a bad reaction."**[16]
>
> *– Brandon Marshall, free agent wide receiver*

Protein, carbohydrates, and fats are part of a healthy meal. A healthy diet helps fuel hard workouts and growing muscles.

control inflammation, it attacks illnesses." Talking about his approach to food, he says, "I look at food as part of the process to being healthy and achieving my goals on the football field."[16]

CARBOHYDRATES

Carbs, which include starches and sugars, are the staple of almost any diet. They are the most energy-packed food source. They fuel athletes on and off the field. Carbohydrates are made of complex molecules that include carbon, hydrogen, and oxygen. The body breaks carbs down into glucose, a type of sugar. Glucose provides cells, tissues, and muscles with the energy they need to function.

Not all carbs are the same, however. Carbs can be divided into two broad groups—complex and simple. The body takes a long time to digest complex carbohydrates. This means that they provide the body with energy for a long period of time. Whole grains are a good source of complex carbs. So are potatoes and some kinds of starchy fruit, such as bananas. Simple carbohydrates, on the other hand, are digested fairly quickly. These include glucose, fructose, and galactose. Foods like candy and cookies are loaded with simple carbs. They'll give the body a short burst of energy as it digests them. But it won't last, and once the calories are burned, a person may feel hungrier and more tired than before. That's why many athletes focus on complex carbs. According to the Mayo Clinic, about 45 to 65 percent of an athlete's calories should come from carbs. This should mainly consist of complex carbs.

Many people group dietary fiber with the carbs. Dietary fiber is material that the body can't digest. It serves an important role in helping the digestive system. It's often included in a food's carb count, but a lot of experts consider dietary fiber to be in its own category.

PROTEIN

Carbs supply the body with energy, but most football players also want to increase their muscle mass. Stronger muscles give them an edge on the field. Protein is the key to muscle growth and repair.

Proteins are molecules made up of chains of amino acids, the building blocks of muscles. Athletes can get protein from meat, nuts, eggs, and dairy products such as milk and yogurt. Many recommend seeking out lean sources of protein, such as fish, chicken, or nuts. Meats such as beef come with high levels of saturated fats. Such foods are high in calories, and the saturated fats they contain can eventually lead to heart disease. A good way to calculate how much protein an athlete should get a day is to multiply weight (in pounds)

Fats can be good and bad for the body. Avocados have good fats.

by 0.75 to find the amount of protein that should be eaten (in grams). This means a 160-pound (73 kg) player should eat about 120 grams of protein per day. This will be approximately 20 to 25 percent of the calories in an athlete's diet.

FATS

The word *fat* is a bad thing to many people. But fat is an important part of any diet. Some important vitamins are fat soluble. It is easier for the body to absorb them when they are eaten with fat. What's important is that you get the right kinds of fat, and in the right amounts. Fats are packed with calories, so correct portions are key.

There are four major groups of fats—saturated, monounsaturated, polyunsaturated, and trans fats. Saturated fats are generally the ones that cause more health problems. They're linked to obesity and heart disease. Saturated fats come mainly from animal products. Most hamburger, for example, is filled with saturated fat. Other foods heavy in saturated fats include butter, whole milk, and ice cream.

Trans fats are especially bad. Most of these are artificial fats. They're found in foods such as margarine, potato chips, and French fries. Partially hydrogenated oils are a main source of trans fats. The US Food and Drug Administration does not consider partially hydrogenated oils safe for use in food.

Athletes need some fat. Most choose to focus on foods that provide polyunsaturated and monounsaturated fats. Salmon, nuts, avocados, and olive oil are all great sources of these relatively healthy fats. They even help protect against heart disease.

VITAMINS AND MINERALS

Nutrition is about more than just calories. The body also needs the right mix of vitamins and minerals. These substances are found in small amounts in food, but they're very important.

Vitamins are nutrients that the body needs to work properly. For example, the body needs the vitamin B2 to help break down food. Vitamin C boosts the immune system, helping it fight off diseases. Each vitamin has its own purpose, and the body needs each of them to be at its best. Many are naturally occurring in the body, while others must be provided by the food people eat. A good and balanced diet will be able to provide people with the vitamins they need.

Minerals are elements and compounds that the body needs. A body is made up almost entirely of four elements—carbon, nitrogen, oxygen, and hydrogen. But it does need small amounts of other elements. Iron, for example, is important in moving oxygen throughout the body. And the body needs calcium to build bones and teeth, clot blood, and do many other things. A lack of calcium can even lead to muscle cramps. Magnesium is needed for many functions in the body, including nerve and muscle function. It can be found in many leafy green vegetables and nuts. Some athletes take a multivitamin or dietary supplements to help them get the vitamins and minerals they need. Multivitamins may help some people, but a balanced and varied diet is a better way of getting these important substances.

HYDRATION

Liquids are just as important as food for athletes. Exercising makes people sweat, causing the body to lose water. Staying hydrated is critical for working out and building muscle. The body needs water to run properly. Sports drinks can be useful in moderate amounts. Most contain substances called electrolytes that replace substances the body loses in sweat. But they often contain a lot of sugar or artificial sweeteners that are not healthful. That's why water should be the first choice for hydration.

Thirst is the body's way of warning of dehydration. When a person is thirsty, the body already needs more water.

> **"I think one of the biggest things is hydration. Just tons and tons of water. . . . It's critical to drink up to make sure you're feeling right."**[17]
>
> *– Russell Wilson, Seattle Seahawks quarterback*

That's why it's key to drink throughout a workout, rather than just at the end. And good hydration isn't just for workouts. Keeping the body well hydrated throughout the day and before practices or games will help an athlete stay at his peak. "I think one of the biggest things is

Players need to make sure to hydrate. Good hydration starts before practices or games.

hydration," says Seattle Seahawks quarterback Russell Wilson. "Just tons and tons of water. . . . It's critical to drink up to make sure you're feeling right."[17]

JUNK FOOD

Almost everyone loves junk food. Whether it's potato chips, candy bars, or donuts, junk food fills the stomach quickly and satisfies cravings. But for an athlete, junk food is usually a bad choice. It fills the body with calories but little nutrition. It can even weigh the athlete down or make him feel bloated. A banana or apple are much better snacks. They will satisfy a sweet tooth while giving the body the nutrients it needs.

Carolina Panthers quarterback Cam Newton has had to learn to cut out junk food. "I used to splurge big," Newton says. "When you're so busy, junk food is too easy to find, especially at night."[18] Newton cut out most of the junk food in his diet and said it made him a leaner, better player. Denver Broncos linebacker Von Miller says he also steers clear of junk food. "When the fourth quarter rolls around, I don't want to be thinking about the ice cream I had the night before," Miller says.[19]

> "When the fourth quarter rolls around, I don't want to be thinking about the ice cream I had the night before."[19]
>
> – Von Miller, Denver Bronco linebacker

PUTTING IT TOGETHER

The world's best football players think about a lot of factors as they eat. They work to fuel their bodies with nutritious foods that give them the energy they need. Everyone's nutrition plan will be different based on their tastes and bodies. Some people have little or no tolerance for gluten. This is a set of proteins found in many grains. Others may have diabetes, a disease that forces them to carefully monitor their sugar intake. Meanwhile, others choose to eat vegetarian or vegan diets, cutting out meats and other animal products. No one plan will work for everyone. Seeing how NFL stars eat is a great start for many young athletes.

Russell Wilson describes a typical day of eating:
Breakfast may look like oatmeal and almond butter. Maybe a protein shake as a mid-morning snack, with some fruit—a one-to-one ratio of carbs and protein. Lunch consists of chicken, rice, and a green vegetable. After practice, I try to have another protein shake. For dinner, good proteins: salmon or steak or

chicken, and vegetables. If I get really hungry at night, I'm in luck, because [my chef] cuts up some great fruits for us.[20]

Wide receiver Brandon Marshall starts his days with egg whites, fruit, cheese, and cereal. For lunch, he focuses on complex carbohydrates and protein. Lunch might be chicken breast, brown rice, and broccoli. Marshall might eat another afternoon meal of chicken and rice. Dinner might include fish, more rice, and a green vegetable such as kale or broccoli. Snacks might include a protein bar and blueberries.

Quarterback Deshaun Watson starts his day with an egg-based breakfast bowl. "For lunch, I aim for a lean protein, some starch, and leafy greens, which are full of magnesium," he says. "Between lunch and dinner, I try and snack on fruit and granola. For dinner, I try to mimic lunch, but with a protein that is also high in omega fatty acids." This might be a fish filet. Watson confesses that he does leave room for a treat now and then. "On game days . . . my guilty pleasure is still sour gummy worms. I still have to have them."[21]

BALL SKILLS

Being in good shape and properly fueled is a good start. It gives players a good base and fuel to make plays. But to make the football team, a player needs to sharpen his skills as well. For players who will handle the football, such as quarterbacks, running backs, wide receivers, and tight ends, ball skills are a must. Properly throwing, catching, and carrying the ball are key to making the team and being successful on the field.

One of the best ways to improve ball skills is by playing catch with a friend. A quarterback might work on throwing accuracy and distance. He can work on placing his throws accurately to where the

BRAIN INJURIES

Football is a dangerous, hard-hitting sport. In recent decades, medical data has shown in great detail the dangers of concussions and other brain injuries. A concussion is bruising to the brain. This type of injury is dangerous. A 2016 study showed that 40 percent of retired NFL players showed some sign of traumatic brain injury. Many believe that young people are at an even greater danger of suffering long-term damage.

A push toward safety has changed the game. It started with improved protective gear, including state-of-the-art helmets designed to soften blows to the head. Rules prohibit certain kinds of hits. Helmet-to-helmet hits on quarterbacks and against defenseless players are both banned. Committing one of these can result in a penalty. In some cases, they can even lead to an ejection from the game. These hits are known to cause concussions. The rules have changed the way defenders must tackle, and this has led coaches and officials at every level of the game to take more care in protecting players from injury.

Yet despite the advances in safety, the fear of brain damage has led some away from the game. Many parents won't let their children play football. Even NFL players worry about the dangers. In 2015, Chris Borland, a rising star at linebacker for the San Francisco 49ers, retired because he feared what might happen. "I just honestly want to do what's best for my health," Borland said. "From what I've researched and what I've experienced, I don't think it's worth the risk. . . . I'm concerned that if you wait [until] you have symptoms, it's too late."

Quoted in "Chris Borland, 24, to Retire from NFL, Cites Fear of Concussions," CNN, March 17, 2015.
www.cnn.com.

receiver can catch them. He can practice hitting targets on the move and throwing short, medium, and long passes. Because players are rarely still or uncovered, practicing leading receivers and placing the ball where only the receiver—and not the defender—can make a play is important.

Receivers also get a lot of benefits from playing catch. They can practice running their routes well and catching passes. Receivers, running backs, and tight ends should all practice catching the ball with their hands. Catching with the arms or body might work when playing catch or in drills, but making a contested catch or holding onto the ball when hit by a defender is much harder. This is a time that players should remember they will play like they practice. Establishing good habits and doing every drill with good technique will translate to doing the same movements in games well too. Coaches take notice when players make consistent, strong catches with the hands.

The basic hand position for catching the football is called the diamond. A player makes a diamond between his hands with the index fingers and thumbs. The player looks through this window to maintain eye contact with the ball all the way to his hands. Keeping eyes on the ball is the most important part of catching a pass.

What about times when a player doesn't have a partner to play catch with? Dallas Cowboys wide receiver Terrance Williams works on his hand strength. Strong hands allow him to snatch the ball out of the air and hold onto it, even when he's being hit. One way to build hand strength is to play catch with yourself. Toss the ball from one hand to the other. Squeeze it tightly for ten seconds, and then toss it back. Squeeze for ten seconds and repeat.

Once a player has the ball, he has to hang onto it. Fumbling the ball is a quick way to get a seat on the bench. Players should practice cradling the ball. They should hold the tip in one hand and have the other tip under their armpit. The rest of the ball should be secured between the forearm and the ribcage. This position is known as high and tight. Players might want to swing their arms when running, but this can lead to carrying the ball away from the body where defenders

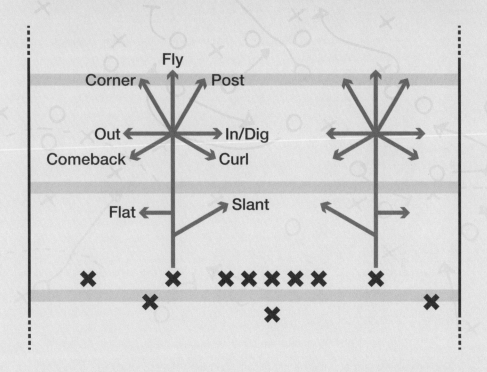

Receivers and quarterbacks need to learn route trees. There are more routes and combination routes, but the basic route tree is a fundamental for every receiver and quarterback. Two receivers' routes can also work together to help each other. Receivers on the same side of the field may both run slants. This forces a safety to choose which corner to help. The receiver without the safety is more likely to get open.

HILLIS SOLVES A PROBLEM

Retired running back Peyton Hillis was one of the NFL's top running backs in 2010 with the Cleveland Browns. He rushed for 1,177 yards and eleven touchdowns—great numbers for a young player. But Hillis also fumbled eight times. He was determined to fix that problem.

Hillis had an unusual solution. During the offseason, he walked around his hometown with a football tucked under his arm. He offered cash to any kid who could knock it out. No one did. And the drill seems to have worked. In ten games during the 2011 season, Hillis fumbled just twice.

can punch it loose. They can practice changing hands while running. And they can work on holding onto the ball as a friend tries to punch it free. Some players carry a ball around with them all day as a constant reminder to never let it go.

Running backs and quarterbacks often go through ball security drills. Running backs might go through drills where coaches try and knock the ball loose. Quarterbacks will be instructed by coaches to keep two hands on the ball and keep it high. Some coaches prefer the quarterback to keep the ball in front of their jersey numbers, while others prefer it to be more toward pad level. A low ball can be more easily swatted by defenders.

Even NFL players need to constantly work on their ball security. In 2015, the San Francisco 49ers practiced it by tickling players while they held the ball. It's not the normal drill for ball security, but it goes to show how important ball security is to coaches.

DEFENSIVE SKILLS

Defensive backs need quickness and agility. They can practice skills such as backpedaling. In a drill called turn and sprint, a player sets up three cones in a straight line. The first cone is the starting point. The second is 5 yards (4.6 m) away. The third is 15 yards (13.7 m) from the start. The player starts at the first cone, with his back to the other cones. He starts the drill by backpedaling to the second cone. Then he plants his foot, turns, and runs toward to the third cone. It's a simple drill, but improving here can pay off when tryouts come.

Defenders must be able to consistently tackle. Good tackling isn't just about hitting as hard as possible. It has more to do with how to hit safely, wrap the arms around a ball carrier, and bring him to the ground. "There are ways to play the game the right way and not be injured," says former NFL safety Donte Whitner. "There's a lot of players out there on defense who think that flying in and diving headfirst is showing toughness. That's not the way to play the game."[22]

The easiest way to practice tackling is with a tackling dummy. One person holds the dummy while the other lines up in a defensive stance. The defender bursts out of his stance and drives into the center of the dummy with his shoulder. The tackler keeps his head up and wraps his arms around the dummy. The holder lets go as the tackler makes contact so that the tackler can drive the dummy to the ground. Oftentimes, tackling with just an arm or a shoulder is not enough to bring down a runner. The Seattle Seahawks use a method called the hawk tackle to emphasize where to contact a ball carrier and wrap him up.

> **"There are ways to play the game the right way and not be injured. There's a lot of players out there on defense who think that flying in and diving headfirst is showing toughness. That's not the way to play the game."[22]**
>
> – Donte Whitner, former strong safety

Practicing tackling with the head up and using correct form ensures that a player will miss fewer tackles. Players can learn about many more drills to sharpen their skills. One good way to set up a training program for tackling is to talk to the team's coaches. They might be able to offer drills that will help.

BLOCKING DRILLS

One of the most difficult skills to practice is blocking. To really practice, a player needs someone else to block. And that means a lot of contact and hitting, which can wear down the body. There are ways to work on blocking technique without any contact, however. One simple way is to practice stances and practice getting up from them as quickly as possible.

Offensive linemen start in three basic stances: the two-point stance, the three-point stance, and the four-point stance. Each point represents a hand or foot on the ground. In a two-point stance, a lineman stands with his knees bent and the body bent slightly at the waist. His arms are in front of his body with the elbows bent. The two-point stance is most useful in passing situations. It allows linemen to react quickly to a pass rusher. It's less useful on running plays, because it's harder to surge forward to drive the defender backward.

The three-point stance is the most commonly used stance. In this stance, linemen stand with one hand on the ground. They bend at the waist and the knees. The lower stance here should flatten the back and raise the hips slightly. Linemen on the right side of the line stand with the right foot behind the left. Linemen on the left side of the line keep their left foot back instead. This allows the lineman to drive off of the front foot when the ball is snapped. The three-point stance is useful in both passing and running plays. It allows the lineman to surge

Linemen need to practice every stance. Each one is useful for different situations in games.

forward or fall back as needed. And it gives the defense no clues as to which sort of play might be coming.

The four-point stance is almost never used in passing situations. In a four-point stance, the lineman stands with both hands on the ground. The player's weight is evenly balanced on the hands and feet. A lineman can keep his body very low when coming out of a four-point stance. That gives him the leverage to drive a defender backward. But it also indicates that a run play is very likely.

Linemen should practice each of these stances, getting comfortable with every style. They can also work on coming out of the stances as quickly and fluidly as possible. They can work on falling back to protect the quarterback or surging forward to drive

Kickers are only called in a few times a game. They have to be able to handle high-stress situations with the game on the line.

back defenders. Performing the technique correctly makes a big difference when it's actually time to get on the field and start hitting.

KICKING AND PUNTING

Kickers and punters practice kicking for distance and accuracy. They also train for flexibility. They may spend much more time on stretching than most other players.

To practice, a kicker or punter needs open space and a lot of footballs. They can also use a kicking net. It's all about repetition. Every kicker has his own motion. But many use the one-and-a-half-step approach. Before each kick, they measure out one and a half steps behind where the ball will be placed. By getting this distance just right, they can consistently and accurately strike the ball each time. Starting too closely will result in kicking under the ball and starting too far away will result in topping the football.

The first step for a kicker is the driving step. It's a long, powerful step. It moves the kicker forward. The driving step gives the kicker the power and momentum he needs to strike the ball solidly. The second step is a short hop step. The kicker brings the kicking foot through the ball, booting it as long and straight as possible. Kickers can practice kicking short and long field goals. Short field goals usually require a higher kick, while long kicks tend to be lower and have a flatter angle.

Punters practice the same way. Most punters use two steps. The first step provides most of the power. It is short because a long step could throw the punter off balance. In the second step, the punter bends the knee of his kicking leg as he brings it forward. He straightens it as it comes into contact with the ball to generate maximum force. Punters practice this to get the timing just right.

Kickers and punters are the biggest part of the kicking game. But they don't do it alone. Long snappers must deliver accurate snaps. They use both hands to give the ball a tight spiral to make it as easy to catch as possible. For place kicks, a holder must receive the ball, place the tip on the ground, and rotate the laces away from the kicker. A bad snap or hold can throw off the kicker's motion.

Every kicker will miss at some point. Part of what makes kickers great is falling back on their practice and mechanics to make the next kick. "I've always been confident in myself and I knew the preparation in practice was going to help and carry me over into games," says Denver Broncos kicker Brandon McManus. "And my rookie year here I struggled a little bit, but one thing I've always held near and dear to my heart is I've never missed two kicks in a row. After a miss, I've always been able to let that go and get to the next kick."[23]

CHAPTER THREE

HOW DO PLAYERS MENTALLY
PREPARE?

Preparing the body is only half of the battle. To succeed on the field, players also need to prepare their minds. "If you want to perform at the highest level, you have to prepare at the highest level mentally," says New England Patriots quarterback Tom Brady.[24]

Every player has his own routine to prepare for game day. Some use visualization to imagine themselves having success. Others dive into game film to gain a mental edge. And some just need to relax and hit the field in a good frame of mind.

VISUALIZATION AND MEDITATION

When the game is on the line, does a player expect to succeed or fail? How a player thinks about what is going to happen can have a big impact on what actually happens. Imagining success does not guarantee a good result, but it can boost the odds. That's why many players turn to techniques such as visualization to train themselves to think positively and expect success.

Visualization is an imaginative exercise. A player imagines himself in specific situations. For example, a kicker might imagine lining up for a game-winning field goal. In his mind, he plays out the steps he must take to make the kick. Then he visualizes the play, focusing on striking

Tom Brady is known for his preparation. He prepares himself mentally and physically.

the ball cleanly and watching it sail through the uprights. A linebacker might visualize an option play by the quarterback. He might imagine seeing how the offensive line moves. He imagines reading the inside hip of the quarterback as he closes in to make the tackle. He imagines the running back catching the option pitch, and he steps wide to drive his shoulder forward to tackle the running back. Running through tough reads and plays can help a player be ready when the situation happens at full speed in a game.

"Visualization has been very important to me," says Green Bay Packers quarterback Aaron Rodgers. "When I have a lot of confidence in a play, as soon as the huddle breaks it's immediately flashing in my head—a picture in my mind for just a millisecond. . . . It's a picture of a play, a successful play, flashing through my mind each time I walk to the line of scrimmage."[25]

There are countless ways to visualize. Many players like to do it in a quiet place. They close their eyes and take deep breaths. They focus on the breaths. This helps to quiet the mind. When they are ready, they start to visualize. Some focus on plays that could be coming. Others focus on memories of past performances. They think about times when they did their absolute best. Reliving these memories again and again helps train the brain to expect success.

Meditation is a similar technique that many players use to calm their minds before a game. Meditation comes in many different forms, but the basic idea is to find a quiet, peaceful place and focus the mind. Some players meditate on calm, peaceful landscapes. Others meditate about football and how they can improve. Cleveland Browns tight end David Njoku watches plays from other great NFL tight ends and then meditates on exactly what each player did to be successful. "I sit down, play some nice music, and meditate and focus on more of my instincts and reactions, imagining defenders when I have the ball in my hands," he says. "I think that really helped me."[26]

> **"Visualization has been very important to me. When I have a lot of confidence in a play, as soon as the huddle breaks it's immediately flashing in my head—a picture in my mind for just a millisecond. . . . It's a picture of a play, a successful play, flashing through my mind each time I walk to the line of scrimmage."[25]**
>
> *– Aaron Rodgers, Green Bay Packers quarterback*

Many players get excited when they make a big play. They have to make sure that the excitement doesn't cost the team a penalty.

These are just some of the ways players can help put themselves in a winning frame of mind. There are countless others. For example, former University of Florida quarterback Chris Leak borrowed a former player's championship ring in the days before he was set to play for his own national title. "[Having the ring] helps to see what you're playing for," he said. "It makes you that much more hungry."[27]

MENTAL TOUGHNESS

Imagining success is a good start. But every football player is also going to face failure. How they deal with it—and learn from it—is a big part of becoming a better player.

Frustration is natural when a player fails. How a player deals with that frustration plays a big role in whether he improves or falls apart.

Many successful players view failure as a chance to learn. They think about why they failed. They may watch film to study their mistakes. And then they work to correct them. A player needs to get comfortable with this, as many coaches have players review the game tape to see what they did right and wrong. If a player doesn't handle correction well, coaches will hesitate to play them.

Sometimes handling mistakes well is easier said than done. Football is an intense game, and emotions run high. But outbursts on the field don't benefit a player's team. Learning to control emotions and look at failure in a constructive way is one of the best ways to get better. The alternative often leads to penalties that hurt a team.

"There's a huge amount of focus about being the best. Sometimes those emotions get the best of [players]," says Dr. Matt Johnson, a sports psychology consultant. He continues,

Part of being a great athlete is learning how to control those emotions and channel those into improving. Sometimes athletes have things going on outside their professional life that may get in the way so they do the best they can to keep those aside and focus on competing. There are game plans. Those are mental skills. Just like physical skills, those are mental skills that need to be practiced. When you practice, you'll see a big difference.[28]

SLEEP

Sleep is key for any athlete. They need both quality and quantity. This is true every night, but especially before a big game or tryout. According to the National Sleep Foundation, teenagers need between eight and ten solid hours of sleep every night. Adults need a bit less. When athletes get enough good sleep, they are sharper, faster, and better able to perform at their peak. When they don't get enough sleep, they go into what is called sleep debt. Sleep debt can leave the mind sluggish. A player will react slower to situations. They may become forgetful or have trouble paying attention. They may be prone to emotional outbursts. And they may grow tired more quickly. All of these effects hurt a player's performance on the football field.

What are the keys to quality sleep? Routine is one of the big ones. Sticking to a consistent bedtime and wake time can help keep players on a healthful sleep schedule. Avoiding stimulants such as caffeine—especially in the afternoon and evening—helps to promote quality sleep. So does limiting blue light exposure before bed. Blue light is the type used in many electronic devices such as tablets, cell phones, and televisions. Many newer phones include night settings that will remove the blue light from screens at a certain time each night. Other factors that can harm sleep include working out before bed and worrying over unfinished tasks such as homework.

"You've gotta have a routine to get your mind and body set so that it's always ready to go when you need it to go," says retired New England Patriots tight end Rob Gronkowski. "I usually like to get to bed around a decent time between eleven and twelve at night. And I get about seven to nine hours of sleep every night and I wake up and start my day from there. I get going by staying active throughout the whole day and getting a workout in."[29]

STUDY

Players who want an extra edge on the field are students of the game. Studying the

> **"You've gotta have a routine to get your mind and body set so that it's always ready to go when you need it to go."[29]**
>
> – Rob Gronkowski, retired New England Patriots tight end

Players need to be in the right place if they want to make the big play. They need to study the playbook to know where to go.

team's playbook helps a player understand his responsibilities on the field and allows him to focus on execution of the play. It's helpful for a player to understand not only his responsibility on each play, but what every other player is supposed to be doing as well.

In 2014, New York Jets rookie tight end Jace Amaro struggled to learn the team's plays. So, he would have another player quiz him with flash cards. Amaro had to respond with all of his responsibilities on the play. It took weeks of work, but Amaro finally mastered the playbook.

Film study is a big deal at the professional and college level, and it's becoming more and more important in the high school game as well. Players can watch and analyze their own game film to see why they succeeded and why they failed. Indianapolis Colts quarterback

Andrew Luck says, "Ask yourself, 'Hey, what did I do wrong? I'm here now. How can I fix my mistakes?' Once you understand where you need to improve . . . you start focusing on what's next."[30]

Many players also watch game film of upcoming opponents. They can learn about the opponents, including: the types of plays and formations they run and what they tend to do. Most players pay special attention to the players they will directly face. For example, a center might watch an opposing nose tackle to see what kind of moves he uses to get around blocks. A cornerback may study an opposing wide receiver to see how he breaks out of routes, where he likes to catch the ball, and how well he holds onto the ball when hit. Having a sense of what an opponent will do gives a player a big leg up and can be the difference between making a big play and making a big mistake. "Proper film study is vital for any NFL team to win," says former NFL player and scout Marc Lillibridge. "Players that can take what they see on the screen and transfer that knowledge to the field will always have their eyes on the prize."[31]

"Everybody in the league is physically gifted and can run fast and jump high," says former Kansas City Chiefs linebacker Derrick Johnson. "What sets you apart is anticipation, knowing where a play is going. . . . Along with team film sessions, I watch film every night at home. I'm looking for tendencies I can exploit and that my whole unit can exploit, especially on third downs."[32]

> **"What sets you apart is anticipation, knowing where a play is going. . . . Along with team film sessions, I watch film every night at home. I'm looking for tendencies I can exploit and that my whole unit can exploit, especially on third downs."**[32]
>
> – Derrick Johnson, former linebacker

TEAMWORK AND LEADERSHIP

Individual preparation is a big part of succeeding at football. But football is a team sport. Each team has eleven players on the field for each play. The team can win only when everyone works together and excels as a unit. "Everyone's job is essential," according to former San Francisco 49ers head coach Bill Walsh. "Everyone has a specific role and specific responsibilities. And each player has to be prepared both mentally and physically to the utmost to play that role."[33]

The biggest way to build teamwork is through practice. For example, a quarterback and a receiver can get to know how the other plays only through playing together. With every route run and pass thrown, they form a stronger connection on the field. The same is true for a long snapper, holder, and place kicker. Offensive linemen practice together to work on communication. They need to know who is blocking whom and what their exact responsibilities are. Linebackers need to know each other's assignments. They also need to know coverages in the secondary so they can communicate with those players. In the same way they need to know coverages, they also need to know the alignment of the defensive line if the linebackers are blitzing. Long snappers, holders, and place kickers must work together and trust each other. If there is a problem, the play breaks down.

Players can also build a sense of team spirit off the field. Many high school teams have specific team-building exercises. They may sit together at the cafeteria during lunch. They may hang out together after practice. Some teams go on overnight retreats with the sole goal of building personal connections between players and coaches. Every little bit helps. The more players work and socialize, the stronger the sense of team they build. Many players and coaches believe that a strong sense of team is key to succeeding on the field.

Leadership is a big part of teamwork. Every team needs leaders, both in the locker room and on the field. Leaders help everyone get on the same page. They drive the other players toward success. Tennessee Titans quarterback Marcus Mariota says that being a leader is about being genuine. "I think it comes down to 'be yourself,'" Mariota says. "Guys will respect that. Guys will gravitate towards that. I don't want to be something that I'm not. Guys tend to pick up on that quickly."[34]

Detroit Lions quarterbacks coach Sean Ryan says that leadership comes naturally to Deshaun Watson. "He's not directing people," Ryan said. "He's telling them, 'Hey, this is what I'm seeing and if you can do this, this is what I think is going to make this work.' You know what I mean? It's his demeanor, it's the way he comes across. You don't feel

Players get ready for the game in the locker room. Each player gets ready in his own way.

like he's telling you what to do. You feel like he's talking football with you and helping you."[35]

There's no one way to be a leader. Some are very vocal. Others lead quietly. They lead by example. But a good leader always tries to stay positive and always works to help teammates be the best that they can be.

GEARING UP FOR GAME DAY

All of a player's preparation—both physical and mental—leads up to one thing: game day. It's when all of a team's hard work is put to the test. And it's critical for every player to be as well prepared as possible to be at his best.

PREGAME RITUALS

Every player gets charged up differently. That's true all the way from high school to the NFL. Some things NFL players do to get ready for games are funny, and some are even strange.

Former Jacksonville Jaguars defensive tackle John Henderson felt that he needed to be woken up before each game. So his pregame ritual was simple. Someone had to slap him in the face—hard—before each game. Henderson believed it was the key to kick-starting his engine. Safety Brian Dawkins would go onto the field and do a series of strange movements, often with a football in hand. At times, Dawkins appeared to be talking to the ball while performing his routine. Legendary Chicago Bears linebacker Brian Urlacher ate two cookies before each game.

For some players, the ritual is doing nothing at all. "I rest. I literally rest," said New England Patriots linebacker Dont'a Hightower. "I don't do anything else. I sit at my locker, I don't listen to music. I don't do anything out of the ordinary. I don't look at film, I don't look at notes. I'm just relaxed. Calm before the storm. I've done enough preparing, I've done enough notes, I've done enough of that stuff during the week. If I don't know it by now, I don't know it. It's not gonna help me last-minute. It's only gonna make me play slower."

It's not just players that have odd routines. Coaches get in on the action too. University of Kansas head coach Les Miles takes a bite out of the field turf before each game. Miles has also been known to chew on a mouthful of grass during high-pressure situations in games.

Quoted in Tom E. Curran, "Patriots Pregame Rituals: Step-by-Step with the Players on Game Day,' NBC Sports, January 20, 2017. www.nbcsports.com.

Every player's routine leading up to game day will be different. Some like to play loud music and get pumped up. Others prefer a quiet, calm space to meditate and collect their thoughts. Some like a pregame meal; others avoid eating before a game. Some want to be in the company of friends, family, or teammates. Others just need some time alone. The trick is for each player to figure out what he

Waking up rested is a key component to getting ready for game day. Players should always make sure to keep their sleep schedule the same before games.

needs to get in the right frame of mind, and then follow the routine that gives him the best chance at success.

Game day preparation really starts the night before a game. Many players choose to eat a calorie-rich meal, often built around complex carbs, to give them a boost of energy for the next day. Sleep is the next big step. Players need to be rested to perform at their peak. They need to make sure they stick to their sleep routines the night before a game, being sure to get eight to ten hours of quality sleep.

"Most NFL players have a similar routine up until they get to the stadium," says former Pro Bowl running back Tiki Barber. He continues,

> They wake up and have a pregame meal. If it's a late game, they will have a meeting to go over game plan, maybe watch some film of the opponent just to remind themselves everything they studied that week as a last minute refresher. Once you get to the stadium, it really depends on . . . personalities. Some guys will sit in the locker room and rock out to whatever music they listen to. Other guys will go out onto the field, run around and get a feel for the environment and motivate themselves by being in the arena they are about to play in.[36]

"I try to do things at the exact same time every week, so I won't have a lot of time to sit there and do nothing," said former San Francisco fullback Fred Beasley. "When I first come in, I read the program—features on players and stuff like that. Then I probably go get some coffee. Then I watch a little football. . . . I don't know if it's really a ritual, but it helps me to do all those things in the same order every time."[37]

As game time approaches, players gear up. Players should prepare the way that helps them play the best. Players should take note of what the coaches have to say and remind themselves what the game plan is. Finding a way to win and also have fun is important.

CHAPTER FOUR

HOW DO PLAYERS PREPARE FOR
THE NEXT LEVEL?

Many high school players dream of playing in college. They may even dream of playing in the NFL one day. How do they give themselves the best chance? There are different routes to the NFL, but most players get there by playing college football. Being a student-athlete is difficult. Players must balance athletics, academics, and their social lives. But whether a player is a backup for a small college or one of the biggest stars in college football, the experience can change them.

"Playing football in college is hard yet extremely rewarding," says former Rutgers University defensive end Myles Jackson:

> **"Football is a lifestyle that requires 100 percent dedication. If you're not in it all the way, you won't succeed and it will be miserable."**[38]
>
> – Myles Jackson, former Rutgers University defensive end

Just getting to this stage is an accomplishment worth noting, and getting through it is an even bigger one. Football is a lifestyle that requires 100 percent dedication. If you're not in it all the way, you won't succeed and it will be miserable. Yes it might be hard and yes you might think there's

Playing at the college level is the next step for some players. It is very different from high school.

no end in sight sometimes. You'll question yourself and wonder if you made the right decision in what school you chose or even if you're good enough to play at all. Once you get through that, though, it's smooth sailing. It's something that you can leverage to do even greater things in life.[38]

THE LEVELS OF COLLEGE FOOTBALL

When players think of college football, they might imagine great teams like the Ohio State Buckeyes, Alabama Crimson Tide, or Clemson Tigers. These are all examples of National Collegiate Athletic Association (NCAA) Division I (DI) programs. DI is the highest level of college football, and the vast majority of NFL players come from these

DI programs such as the University of Oregon will have nicer stadiums and scholarships than smaller DII and DIII programs. Players need to take the whole program into consideration when deciding where to play.

programs. But it's not the only way to play college football. Division II and III (DII and DIII) also offer a high level of play for student-athletes. And many players attend smaller schools that are members of the National Association of Intercollegiate Athletics (NAIA), often considered a step below DIII.

In general, DI schools have the biggest budgets, the most scholarships available, and the best facilities. Games are often broadcast on national television, giving players the maximum exposure. Most—but not all—DI athletes receive athletic scholarships that pay for all or part of their educational expenses.

DII schools also offer some scholarships. But their overall budgets tend to be much smaller, and NCAA rules limit how much scholarship money they can award. As a result, many DII athletes receive partial or no athletic scholarships, although some bridge that gap with grants and

academic scholarships. DIII schools cannot offer athletic scholarships, so student-athletes must look for other ways of paying for their schooling and expenses. NAIA schools may offer some athletic scholarship money, but it varies by school.

Because the most scholarship money and exposure is available at the DI level, that's where top players prefer to play. But sometimes a top recruit isn't academically eligible to play at DI schools. In this situation, he may spend a year or two at a junior college before transferring to a new program.

The lower ranks produce plenty of NFL talent as well. In 2013, DII Minnesota State University, Mankato wide receiver Adam Thielen attended a Minnesota Vikings open tryout. Thielen impressed Viking coaches and received an invitation to training camp. He made the team, playing mostly on special teams for his first two seasons. In 2016, Thielen's third NFL season, he broke out as an offensive star. He went on to become one of the top receivers in the NFL. He started at a DII school on a $500 scholarship—not even enough money to cover his books. "I never thought, 'One day I'm going to be an NFL receiver,'" Thielen says. "I just take it one day at a time, and have fun doing it."[39]

ACADEMICS

When it comes to preparing for college football, a player's performance on the field is only part of the job. The NCAA and each college have their own standards for academics as well. If a player isn't doing his schoolwork and getting the grades he needs, he'll never even make it onto a college football field.

It can be hard to balance games, practices, workouts, team meetings, and academics. High school sports take up a lot of student-athletes' time and energy. Yet they still have to do their schoolwork and keep up their grades. How do they do it? The trick is good organization and time management. Student-athletes need to make a habit out of using their downtime to do school work. That can come during study hall periods, on the school bus, or on weekends. They try not to put things off and fall behind. And many of them use school resources such as tutors to help them stay on top of their homework.

> **"It's about whether or not you're going to be successful when you show up on campus. It's about being the very best you, in every way possible."**[40]
>
> – *Mike MacIntyre, University of Mississippi defensive coordinator*

"[High school players] are in total control of their effort in the classroom, their behavior off the field, and their intensity on the field," says Mike MacIntyre, defensive coordinator at the University of Mississippi. He continues,

When you see a young man taking care of business in those three areas, you will find that he's probably reaching his potential as a football player, as well. That's ultimately what catches the attention of a college coach and what gets you recruited. The whole key to this is not the actual process of recruiting. It's about whether or not you're going to be successful when you show up on campus.

It's about being the very best you, in every way possible. And, having those three characteristics already developed as a high schooler means you're most likely going to have success at the next level. That's what really matters.[40]

The academic demands carry on into college. Players must keep up an academic standard to remain eligible to play. Some take light course loads during the football season and then make up for it with heavier loads during the off-season or over the summer. And most schools offer at least some course credit for intercollegiate athletics. Athletes also have access to academic services and tutors that can work with their unusual and busy schedules. But this doesn't mean the workload or responsibilities get any easier.

THE RECRUITING PROCESS

What happens when a high school player is good enough to attract attention from college programs? It's time for the recruiting process to begin. Recruitment is how colleges try to build teams. Head coaches and other staff members write letters, make phone calls, and visit possible future players, all with the hope of bringing them into the program.

Performance on the field is a big part of what gets a player recruited. But it's not the only factor. NCAA rules set strict guidelines on how colleges recruit players. For DI schools, coaches can begin to contact players electronically on September 1 of their junior year. That includes texts, emails, and social media messaging. DII coaches get a bit of a head start. They can start recruiting on June 15. DIII and NAIA coaches don't have any limits on when they can start recruiting. Similar rules spell out when coaches can call or visit a player and how often they are allowed to contact each player.

Many players attend football camps to check out a program. This also lets the coaches take a closer look at how players perform in drills.

The more serious recruiting starts in April of a player's junior year. That's when players can make their first campus visit. Coaches, current players, and staff members show them the campus, the football facilities, and the surrounding area. In total, a player is allowed to make five official visits to DI college campuses. Universities pay for official visits. However, there are no limits at lower levels, and many players make unofficial visits on their own.

The final stage of recruiting is commitment. That's when a player announces which college he will attend. There are several ways a player can do this. One is with a verbal commitment. This is when a player announces his choice. A verbal commitment is not binding. Other colleges can continue to recruit the player, and the player is allowed to change his mind.

A more formal commitment is the signing of a National Letter of Intent. When a player signs this letter, he is closing off the recruiting process. Other schools can no longer contact him. This cannot be signed earlier than December 19 of a player's senior year for recruits signing with a DI or DII program. This is the early signing period. The National Signing Day is the beginning of the regular signing period and is February 6 of their senior year. The National Letter of Intent assures a player of scholarship money for at least one year—as long as he meets the school's requirements to enter. Most players go on to attend the school with which they sign a National Letter of Intent. However, if they do change their minds after signing, they can request a release from the agreement. In most cases, schools will grant the release. The coaches may not want to lose the player, but they also don't want to build a team with students who do not want to be there.

WHAT CAN PLAYERS DO IF THEY'RE NOT RECRUITED?

What happens when players enter their junior year and don't hear from any college coaches? It's time to get to work. Many players put together videos of their game highlights. They send the tapes to schools that they think might be interested. Some players send the tapes to dozens of programs. Others use a more targeted approach. They research schools and their current football rosters, seeking out programs they believe they have the best chance to help. For example, a dual-threat quarterback might seek out a school whose coach uses mobile quarterbacks. Or he might search for schools with few quarterbacks on the active roster. Checking a program's current commitments also plays a role in where players sign. Players also attend camps held at universities where they would like to play.

This gives coaches the opportunity to see the player up close and get to know him.

If sending videos and going to camps does not get a response, it might be time to look at lower levels. Players can seek out DII, DIII, NAIA, or junior college programs. Similarly, students who failed to get the grades needed to qualify for a DI program may turn to junior college for a year or two. They can continue to develop their skills while also gaining academic eligibility.

SCHOLARSHIPS

A player who joins a college team may or may not receive an athletic scholarship. A scholarship is money granted to a student-athlete to pay his or her educational expenses. According to the NCAA, DI and DII colleges give a combined $2.9 billion in athletic scholarships to about 150,000 student-athletes across all sports each year.

Not all scholarships are created equally. Full scholarships, sometimes called full rides, pay for all expenses. They cover tuition, room and board, and books. These types of scholarships are most common at DI schools. Many more students receive partial scholarships. These cover just a portion of the student's expenses. For example, wide receiver Adam Thielen's scholarship was just $500.

Some players join a football team without any scholarship at all. These players are called walk-ons. If a walk-on can impress the coaching staff, however, he may be rewarded with a scholarship in the future. One of the most famous walk-on football players in recent times was quarterback Baker Mayfield. Mayfield started his college career in 2013 at Texas Tech University as a walk-on. He later transferred as a walk-on again for the University of Oklahoma. He went on to win the Heisman Trophy in 2017 and was the top pick in

THE PAY-TO-PLAY DEBATE IN COLLEGE ATHLETICS

In recent years, the debate over how college athletes are compensated has grown. Schools and conferences make hundreds of millions of dollars in ticket sales, merchandise sales, and television contracts. But the athletes on the field don't see any of that money, beyond what their scholarships provide. They're not even allowed to make money by marketing their own name and fame. They can be suspended even for charging a fee or accepting a gift in exchange for an autograph.

Many people believe this is wrong. In 2014, players on the Northwestern University football team petitioned to form a labor union. Their bid failed, but it helped kick-start renewed discussion about paying college athletes. Supporters argue that players give far more to universities than they receive in return, and that they should be paid for the money they help bring in. Opponents argue that paying college athletes would make the college ranks little different than the pros, and that smaller schools with less funding would be unable to compete.

the 2018 NFL Draft. The Heisman Trophy is awarded to the top DI football player every year. It is mostly awarded to quarterbacks and running backs. Other notable NFL players who started as walk-ons include Patriots kicker Stephen Gostkowski, Detroit Lions defensive end Ezekiel Ansah, Washington cornerback Josh Norman, and Green Bay Packers linebacker Clay Matthews.

"[Not getting any scholarship offers is] definitely something that motivates me, but it's not like I'm dwelling on the past," Matthews says. "I let everyone know that it's not your typical college career but I wouldn't change it for anything because I think if I had it easier in regard to going to college and being handed certain things then I might not be where I am today or have the same type of drive or intensity that fuels me each and every day."[41]

PLAYING COLLEGE FOOTBALL

Players generally get four years of eligibility in college football. But that doesn't mean all of them play for four years. Some incoming freshmen are given redshirt status. A redshirt is a player who practices with the team but plays in four or fewer games that season. A redshirt player does not lose a year of his eligibility. Instead, he has a chance to build his skills and focus on academics. Players who play their freshman year can save that redshirt year for later in their career if they need it. Players can also get redshirt status because of injuries.

Some players leave the team before their four years are complete. An injury may end their career. They may find that they don't enjoy the game anymore, or they aren't good enough to compete. Some of the very best players leave the team after their junior or redshirt sophomore year to enter the NFL Draft. For all of these reasons, a college football roster is constantly changing. Players who stay with the program are always facing new challenges and opportunities.

NCAA rules place strict limitations on players. Colleges are allowed to offer players money for school expenses only. They cannot pay players in any other way, and neither can the school's boosters or supporters. These rules are to keep a level playing field for all schools. But they can create hardships for players. Players cannot accept gifts over a certain value. They are limited in what kinds of jobs they can take. Breaking these rules can result in penalties for the player and the school.

ENTERING THE NFL: FROM THE COMBINE TO THE DRAFT

For the top college prospects, being selected high in the NFL Draft is often likely. Most others have to show off their skills. Their college

Players who attend the NFL Draft, such as Von Miller, can go up on stage if they are selected. But some players prefer to stay home with their family during the draft.

performance—especially in their final year or two—is a big part of their NFL resume. But it doesn't end there.

Some players are invited to exhibition games such as the Senior Bowl or Shrine Game. These games are designed to showcase the talent of NFL prospects. Players also visit teams for private workouts and interviews.

One of the biggest events leading up to the NFL Draft is the NFL Scouting Combine. The Combine is an invitation-only, week-long showcase for NFL prospects. Players are grilled in interviews. NFL scouts and coaches test their intelligence, emotional maturity, and physical skills in a series of drills. Players are grouped by positions, measured, and then run through different drills designed to measure certain skills for each position. Players must show off their size, speed,

AARON RODGERS:
FROM JUNIOR COLLEGE TO THE NFL

NFL fans know Aaron Rodgers as one of the best quarterbacks in the world. But that wasn't always the case. When Rodgers was a sophomore in high school, he stood just 5 feet, 6 inches (1.7 m) tall. He was a skilled passer, but his small size made major colleges overlook him. Even after a growth spurt as a senior, not one DI college offered Rodgers a scholarship.

So Rodgers agreed to attend Butte Community College, a junior college. He went on to win the starting job and broke several of the school's passing records. That was enough to catch the attention of coaches at the University of California (Cal). They visited Rodgers and quickly offered him a scholarship. Rodgers jumped at the chance. He played two seasons for Cal. After his junior season, he left Cal to enter the NFL Draft. The Green Bay Packers selected him with the 24th pick in the first round, and Rodgers went on to become one of the best quarterbacks in the NFL. He could have given up football when no one recruited him in high school. Instead, he took the only opportunity he was offered and made himself an NFL star.

jumping ability, agility, and in-game skills. A good performance can boost a player's draft stock, while a poor one can send them spiraling down teams' draft boards.

Beyond the Combine, players often have pro days held at their program's facilities. These are like a combine, but any player can have one. A pro day allows players to run through drills with players they are familiar with. They can try a second time for a new personal best in some of the measured exercises, such as the bench press, 40-yard (37-m) dash, vertical leap, and broad jump. Sometimes scouts ask players to perform extra drills or run certain routes.

Next comes the NFL Draft. It's a three-day event in which NFL teams take turns selecting incoming players, with a lot of wheeling and dealing by teams. Many of the top prospects attend the draft, where they are called up onto the stage to pose for photographs when selected. Others stay at home, waiting for a phone call.

It can be a rough wait. In 2000, Michigan quarterback Tom Brady stayed at home with his family, waiting to be picked. He watched as round after round passed with no phone calls from NFL teams. As the fifth round came and went, Brady grew restless. He left the house and went for a walk with his parents. Finally, in the sixth round, the New England Patriots called. They selected Brady with the 199th overall pick in the draft. Two years later, Brady led the Patriots to a Super Bowl title, and he went on to help build one of the NFL's most successful dynasties.

WHAT HAPPENS TO PLAYERS WHO AREN'T DRAFTED?

Drafted players aren't guaranteed a spot on an NFL roster, but they have a big advantage heading into training camp. Still, teams invite undrafted players to join them for minicamps and training camp, and every year several undrafted rookies manage to make an impact. Among the best undrafted players in NFL history are James Harrison, Kurt Warner, Jeff Saturday, Adam Thielen, Warren Moon, Antonio Gates, John Randle, and Tony Romo.

What happens to players who don't make an NFL roster? It's not over. Some join practice squads. Each team carries a handful of young players who practice with the team but cannot play in games. They try to hone their skills and earn a roster spot for the following season.

Others must look for other opportunities. The NFL is not the only professional football league. Many players take their talents to the

Canadian Football League (CFL) or the Arena Football League (AFL). Players in these leagues generally don't earn nearly as much money as NFL players. But they can earn a living playing the game they love, with the hopes that they might impress NFL teams and still take that step. Hall of Fame quarterback Warren Moon won five CFL championships, known as the Grey Cup, before getting the call to the NFL. Defensive end Cameron Wake spent two seasons in the CFL.

Meanwhile, Kurt Warner made his name in the AFL and European Football League before finally getting an NFL shot. Warner says that even in the hard times, he never stopped believing in himself. "I sat on the bench for four years in college, but the one year I played I was Player of the Year in my conference," he said. "Then I went to Arena Football. I played three years. I was in the championship game twice and was voted the best quarterback in Arena Football during my time there. I went to Europe for a year, was the best quarterback statistically in the one year that I played there."[42] Warner kept waiting for his shot, and when he finally got it, he went on to become a Hall of Fame quarterback.

Still, for every player who does find a career in professional football, there are dozens who never get the chance. That's why education is so important. College football players need something to fall back on, and a college degree is a great way to plan for a

> **"I value a lot of things in my life, including education. I now have a degree, and nobody can take that away from me. It was very important to me to become a college graduate—not for anyone else, but for myself."[43]**
>
> *– Cam Newton, Carolina Panthers quarterback*

future outside of football. NFL players will retire someday, and their college degrees will help guide the direction of their lives after football. "I wanted to finish something I started," said Carolina Panthers quarterback Cam Newton after completing his college degree. "I value a lot of things in my life, including education. I now have a degree, and nobody can take that away from me. It was very important to me to become a college graduate—not for anyone else, but for myself."[43]

Tennessee Titans quarterback Marcus Mariota lists earning his college degree as his greatest achievement. "I understand that football is only a certain time in my life, and my degree will help me sustain my life well past football," he said. "I was so proud of that, and the amount of work I put into it."[44]

Not every player will get the chance to play in college or the NFL. But every high school player can enjoy his time playing the game he loves. Working hard and enjoying the game happens at every level. Players should work hard, but they should also enjoy that they get to play the game.

SOURCE NOTES

INTRODUCTION: HOW DO PLAYERS MAKE THE TEAM?

1. Quoted in Matthew Jussim, "NFL Training: The Eternal Youth of Larry Fitzgerald," *Men's Journal*, n.d. www.mensjournal.com.

2. Quoted in Luke O'Neil, "How to Work Out—and Eat—Like an NFL Linebacker," *Esquire*, August 3, 2016. www.esquire.com.

3. Quoted in Matt Weston, "Deshaun Watson's Diet: How It's Changed Since He Entered the NFL," *SB Nation Battle Red Blog*, May 3, 2018. www.battleredblog.com.

4. Quoted in Zameena Mejia, "Tom Brady's 4 Mental Tricks for Success," *CNBC*, February 3, 2018. www.cnbc.com.

5. Ryan Riddle, "How an NFL Player Prepares for Training Camp," *Bleacher Report*, July 2, 2013. www.bleacherreport.com.

6. Quoted in Ali Montag, "This Mental Exercise Is NFL Star Richard Sherman's Secret to Success," *CNBC*, February 2, 2018. www.cnbc.com.

7. Quoted in Sam Dehority, "Workout Advice from Clay Matthews: How to Be a Better Athlete," *Men's Journal*, n.d. www.mensjournal.com.

CHAPTER ONE: HOW CAN PLAYERS PREPARE FOR TRYOUTS?

8. Quoted in Yoni Blumberg, "How This NFL Linebacker Uses His Bathroom Wall for a Goal-Setting Exercise," *CNBC*, February 4, 2018. www.cnbc.com.

9. Quoted in Dave Golokhov, "Beauty and the Beast: NFL Linebacker DeMarcus Ware," *AskMen.com*, n.d. www.askmen.com.

10. Quoted in Kevin Clark, "Why the 49ers Love to Stretch," *Wall Street Journal*, January 16, 2013. www.wsj.com.

11. Quoted in Matthew Jussim, "How Russell Wilson Trains to Build Super Bowl Strength," *Men's Journal*, n.d. www.mensjournal.com.

12. Dhani Jones, "Pushing the Limits," *The Players' Tribune*, April 8, 2016. www.theplayerstribune.com.

13. Quoted in Eric Campitelli, "Chip Kelly No Longer Tracking Eagles' Sleep with Wearables," *NBC Sports*, November 20, 2015. www.nbcsports.com.

14. Quoted in Dane Brugler, "John Ross Breaks 40-Yard Dash Record at Combine with 4.22-Second Run," *SportsDay*, March 4, 2017. sportsday.dallasnews.com.

15. Quoted in Nancy Churmin, "Advice on Making the Team from High School Coaches," *Dallas Morning News*, August 2010. www.dallasnews.com.

CHAPTER TWO: HOW CAN PLAYERS PREPARE THEIR BODIES?

16. Quoted in Matthew Jussim, "Brandon Marshall's Lean, Mean Nutrition Plan for Losing Weight," *Men's Journal*, n.d. www.mensjournal.com.

17. Quoted in Emily Abbate, "The Real-Life Diet of Russell Wilson, Who Plans to Play Football Until He's 45," *GQ*, September 17, 2018. www.gq.com.

18. Quoted in Lara Rosenbaum, "Cam Newton's Top-Secret Nutrition Plan," *Men's Health*, July 23, 2012. www.menshealth.com.

19. Quoted in Scott Davis, "Super Bowl MVP Von Miller Cut Out Red Meat, Sports Drinks, and Junk Food in the Offseason to Terrorize Quarterbacks Even More," *Business Insider*, February 7, 2016. www.businessinsider.com.

20. Quoted in Abbate, "The Real-Life Diet of Russell Wilson."

21. Quoted in Matt Weston, "Deshaun Watson's Diet: How It's Changed Since He Entered the NFL," *SB Nation Battle Red Blog*, May 3, 2018. www.battleredblog.com.

22. Quoted in Chris Strauss, "49ers' Donte Whitner: 50% of NFL Players Don't Tackle Properly," *USA Today*, January 30, 2013. www.usatoday.com.

23. Quoted in "NFL Kickers Discuss Misses, Pressure and Job Security," *ESPN*, September 21, 2018. www.espn.com.

CHAPTER THREE: HOW DO PLAYERS MENTALLY PREPARE?

24. Quoted in Zameena Mejia, "Tom Brady's 4 Mental Tricks for Success," *CNBC*, February 3, 2018. www.cnbc.com.

25. Quoted in David Fleming, "Rodgers: 'I'm Trying to Break Old Habits,'" *ESPN*, December 1, 2011. www.espn.com.

26. Quoted in Lorenzo Reyes, "Draft Prospect David Njoku Uses Meditation to Help Him Improve as a TE," *USA Today*, April 21, 2017. www.usatoday.com.

27. Quoted in Associated Press, "Leak Borrows Championship Ring for Motivation," *ESPN*, January 5, 2007. www.espn.com.

28. Quoted in Kevin Casas, "Can Sore Losers Erode the Pro Sports Landscape?" *Fort Worth Star-Telegram*, August 26, 2017. www.star-telegram.com.

29. Quoted in Courtney Connley, "Rob Gronkowski Gets 7 to 9 Hours of Sleep Each Night—Here's the Rest of His Routine," *CNBC*, October 21, 2018. www.cnbc.com.

30. Quoted in Andrew Daniels, "Going Deep with Andrew Luck," *Men's Health*, November 22, 2013. www.menshealth.com.

31. Marc Lillibridge, "A Former Player's Perspective on Film Study and Preparing for an NFL Game," *Bleacher Report*, November 29, 2012. www.bleacherreport.com.

32. Quoted in Dan Roe, James Nosek, Brielle Gregory, and Ben Court, "Yoga, Pedialyte, and the Movie 300: How 6 NFL Players Prep for Sunday," *Men's Health*, September 8, 2016. www.menshealth.com.

33. Quoted in Richard Rapaport, "To Build a Winning Team: An Interview with Head Coach Bill Walsh," *Harvard Business Review*, January–February 1993. www.hbr.org.

34. Quoted in Kevin Clark, "The Collected Stories of Marcus Mariota," *The Ringer*, September 5, 2017. www.theringer.com.

35. Quoted in Cameron Wolfe and Sarah Barshop, "Leaders from the Start: Deshaun Watson, Marcus Mariota are 'Guys You Want to Follow,'" *ESPN*, September 29, 2017. www.espn.com.

36. Tiki Barber, "Former NHL Running Back Tiki Barber on What Game Day Is Like for Players," *Huffington Post*, October 3, 2014. www.huffpost.com.

37. Quoted in "NFL Players in Their Own Words," *HowStuffWorks*, December 7, 2003. entertainment.howstuffworks.com.

CHAPTER FOUR: HOW DO PLAYERS PREPARE FOR THE NEXT LEVEL?

38. Myles Jackson, "What's It Like to Play NCAA Division I Football?" *Slate*, February 24, 2014. www.slate.com.

39. Quoted in Jon Nowacki, "Former DII Receiver Adam Thielen Finding Success in NFL," *NCAA.com*, November 20, 2017. www.ncaa.com.

40. Quoted in "College Recruiting Q&A with Colorado Football Coach Mike MacIntyre," *Playced*, April 23, 2018. www.playced.com.

41 Quoted in Seth Gruen, "The GQA: Clay Matthews," *GQ*, November 11, 2011. www.gq.com.

42. Quoted in Bob Baum, "Warner Took Improbable Journey to the Hall of Fame," *Belleville News-Democrat*, August 4, 2017. www.bnd.com.

43. Quoted in Steve Helling, "NFL Quarterback Cam Newton Gets His College Degree: I Promised My Mom I Would Finish," *People*, June 2, 2015. www.people.com.

44. Quoted in Andrew Daniels and David J. Phillip, "Marcus Mariota Talks about the NFL Draft, Tinder, and Literally Being a Meathead," *Men's Health*, April 23, 2015. www.menshealth.com.

BOOKS

Matt Doeden, *The College Football Championship: The Fight for the Top Spot*. Minneapolis: Millbrook Press, 2016.

Rebecca Koehn, *Behind the Scenes of Pro Football*. North Mankato, MN: Capstone Press, 2019.

Dan Myers, *Make Me the Best Football Player*. Minneapolis, MN: Abdo Publishing, 2017.

Rachel Stuckey, *Be a Force on the Field: Skills, Drills, and Plays*. New York: Crabtree Publishing Company, 2016.

John Walters, *Inside High School Football: A Changing Tradition*. Broomall, PA: Mason Crest, 2017.

INTERNET SOURCES

Jessica Clifford and K. Maloney, "Quick Facts. . ." *Colorado State University Extension*, December 2010. extension.colostate.edu.

Michael Gauthier, "Strength & Weight Training for High School Football," *LiveStrong*, n.d. www.livestrong.com.

Brandon Hall, "5 Athletic Attributes that Elite Pass Rushers Have in Common," *Stack*, January 26, 2017. www.stack.com.

Dan Peterson, "How to Make the Game Slow Down: Football IQ," *USA Football*, August 20, 2013. www.blogs.usafootball.com.

WEBSITES

NCAA.com

www.ncaa.com

The official site of the NCAA has the latest news in college sports, as well as rules and guidelines college athletes and coaches must follow.

NFL

http://nfl.com

The official site of the NFL has all of the latest news on NFL teams and players.

Pro Football Reference

www.pro-football-reference.com

Learn more about every NFL player, their stats, history, college careers, and game-by-game performance.

Rivals

https://n.rivals.com

Rivals is one of the top resources for information on high school football teams and players. Read features, game reports, and scouting reports on all the top prospects.

USA Football

www.usafootball.com

USA Football is an online reference for youth football coaches, offering tips, drills, and online courses.

INDEX

INDEX CONTINUED

IMAGE CREDITS

ABOUT THE AUTHOR

Matt Scheff is an artist and author living in Alaska. He enjoys mountain climbing, deep-sea fishing, and curling up with his two Siberian huskies to watch football.